DISCOVERING. BECOMING. FULFILLING!

DEMYSTIFYING THE CONCEPT OF
SELF-ESTEEM FOR WOMEN

ANDRINE TULLOCH-FRANCIS

Extra MILE Innovators
Kingston, Jamaica W.I.

. . . . .

Published by

Extra MILE Innovators

54 Montgomery Avenue,

Kingston 10, Jamaica W.I.

www.extramileja.com

Editor: Nicola Brown

Cover Design and Illustrations:

Temiloluwa Adeoye | tm.designx@gmail.com

Author Contact: For conferences, workshops, seminars and reader feedback, contact the author at atullochfrancis2@gmail.com.

NOTES

I dedicate this book to my parents, Lascelle and Avis Tulloch.

For the way you nurtured me, ensuring that I displayed confidence at all times.
For every encouraging word and all the exposure, even from a very young age.
For the times I felt I could not make it, you both always knew the right actions to take. For this, I am truly grateful. I love you both so much!

Endorsements

Timely, relevant, appropriate and inspiring are just a few adjectives I would use to describe this amazing piece of work that will become an international bestseller. It was such a pleasure reading it. The layout and flow of the content, interspersed with anecdotes and exercises, makes it a fitting book for the Professional Development programme across the Caribbean and should be on the book list for schools. I'm looking forward to the version for young men.

Self-esteem issues, as Andrine rightly argues, are widespread and impact a wide cross section of persons, from pre-teens to retired adults. This book applies to all these groups and I encourage everyone to engage with the material meaningfully. It can save lives and propel people to greatness. For those who teach self-esteem to any age group, this is very practical and easy to read. The exercises are appropriately placed and the step-by-step guide is easy to apply. I'll definitely be recommending this book to those who take part in my Self-Esteem workshops.

The strength of this book lies in the spiritual/scriptural foundation which anchors the lessons. During the writing of this book Andrine was no doubt anointed and inspired, and so her work is richly inspiring.

Blessings in overflow as you expand your horizons to reach a wider global audience.

—Dr. Nsombi Jaja,
CMC, PMP, SMC, SAMC

. . . . .

In this age of increased connectivity and information overload, women and girls are bombarded with images of what they should be. To exacerbate the pressure females face, there are also societal and cultural norms which do nothing to elevate them. With such a weight of complex issues weighing our women down, this book is a timely piece, offering a refreshing and simple guide for training females to elevate their morale.

The author shares comical stories from her personal experiences coupled with research-based best practices to empower our demoralized women. Anchoring the entire book is the Word of God, embedded in every useful tip given. Each chapter strategically includes resonating inspirational thoughts, reflection questions and gripping anecdotes, which act as practical tools for constructing a positive self-image. As the author teaches our women to value themselves, she allows for real-time introspection and decision-making with the smoothness of a skilled educator. Each page shows us we all stand to benefit from becoming and being around confident, purpose-driven women.

—Candice Allen
Foreign Language
Bilingual Education & ESOL Teacher

"Discovering. Becoming. Fulfilling!" masterfully written by Andrine Tulloch-Francis is a chest of unsearchable treasure. The personal style of the writer made it an easy read. Each page, etched with simple language, carries profound truths that I found to be refreshing and empowering. Having struggled with low self-esteem in the past, I could easily relate to the content and identify the usefulness of each step outlined.

Andrine challenges readers to break from the self-sabotaging thoughts that have caged them into a place of mediocrity and a "less-than" existence. This book is a powerful reminder of the divine value within me. It reminded me of the need to be intentional in defining my place on earth and valuing the unique gifts and talents that God wants me to use in the advancement of His kingdom.

Having read this book, I feel ready to walk in boldness, unashamed to celebrate me, the Imago Dei, and free to celebrate the successes of others with no fear of fading in their light. Thank you for this, Andrine.

—Roshelle S. Jackson

Guidance Counsellor, St. Hugh's High School

Foreword

 I wish to commend and congratulate Andrine Tulloch-Francis, the author of this book, "Discovering, Becoming, Fulfilling! Demystifying the Concept of Self-Esteem for Women."

Andrine and I are contemporaries in the field of education. I met her through my husband, Andrew Norman, and later got to know her better, as she served as a Teacher Representative and Counsellor for Passion and Purity, a Youth Movement founded by Andrew and myself.

You may agree that God created everyone with a purpose, but there are several factors which may prevent us from discovering His purpose in the time He has given us on earth.

One of these things is an unhealthy view of ourselves or what we call low self-esteem. This is the issue that Andrine tackles through carefully crafted sentences, meant to inspire readers towards self-appreciation and confidence.

Andrine uses scriptural principles to guide women to discover what God says about them, to stimulate their thinking and encourage them to embrace the way God sees them. Using anecdotal references, some of her personal experiences, and the experiences of other persons who have successfully overcome these challenges, the writer shares needful insights to illustrate important truths and identify the factors which prevent women from becoming who God created them to be.

The Word of God reminds us in Proverbs 23:7(NKJV) that, "For as he thinks in his heart, so is he." I found this book to be enlightening, interesting and insightful, and I believe this theme is relevant for women today. I am confident that it will inspire the readers to develop a healthier view of themselves as they discover and express the purpose for which God, in His wisdom, has created and compacted in them.

—Donnette Norman
Minister of the Gospel, Educator
Founder and President
Christian Teachers in Action

Table of Contents

"Self-esteem isn't everything; it's just that there's nothing without it."
—Gloria Steinem

For I can do everything through Christ, who gives me strength."
—Philippians 4:13 (NLT)

Introduction

"Self-esteem is how we value ourselves;
it's an essential requirement for us to thrive—to have
normal healthy development. It's how we perceive our
value to the world and how valuable we think we are
to others." —Karen Chaston, Co-Founder,
Live Love by Design

Self-esteem affects every facet of our lives. Simply put, it is having good thoughts about one's self. While it may appear easy enough, this topic has been the center of many discussions for years, because not everyone has (or knows how to have) a positive self-esteem, especially in the 21st century.

As an educator at the secondary school level since September 2005, I have come in contact with many persons who suffer from low self-esteem. Currently, I am at an all girls' school and the evidence of low self-esteem, or sometimes, no self-esteem, seems to be very glaring. Concurrently, on the global scale, it concerns me to see the number of persons who do not seem to value themselves. They often display self-defeating behaviours; linked to how they perceive themselves and further affect the success they experience.

Studies have shown that self-esteem is one factor that helps to contribute to a better version of one's self. Baumeister et al. 2003 concludes that the benefits of high self-esteem fall into two categories: enhanced initiative and pleasant feelings. Chaston, in exploring this topic, states that the strongest factor for success is having positive self-esteem, reinforced through three (3) key actions:

Believing you can do it.
Believing you deserve it.
Believing you will get it.

Once this becomes habitual, you find that success is within your reach. But getting to this stage also requires a firm stance in always having God as your guide. Righteousness produces boldness, confidence in who you are spiritually, emotionally and intellectually. Doing all we can to the glory of God can be the greatest feat of any person.

Anecdote

There was a brilliant student who attended my church occasionally. Let's call her Anissa. I recall asking her to take part in a church concert and she accepted. The day came and though she did fairly well, her nerves, coupled with her self-doubt, hadn't allowed her talent to shine. She lacked confidence.

Years went by and I had the pleasure of a chance meeting. This time, it was at a graduation. She was the valedictorian.

From the beginning of her speech and throughout, I was completely transfixed. Her delivery and presentation were outstanding. There were many parts in the speech where she sang so confidently and effortlessly. It was so different from the young lady who sang at the concert back at church. Her mannerisms and carriage had changed, and she had matured as a young lady. I believe the source was developing a positive self-esteem. She now believed she could do it, believed she deserved it, and so she got it.

I was and still am proud of this young lady.

Introspection

It is often said that, "For as he thinks in his heart, so is he" (Proverbs 23:7, NKJV). What thoughts do you harbour about yourself? This book provides 14 habits to develop and help improve your self-esteem.

I hope this book will yield positive outcomes, somehow serving as a blueprint for building and maintaining positive self-esteem.

Enjoy and be inspired to be the best version of you.

Part 1:
Building Self-Esteem

Step 1:
YOU Are Fearfully and Wonderfully Made

D o you believe that God has a plan for your life? Do you believe that only you can fulfill His plan for your life?

Your uniqueness and idiosyncrasies are all a part of God's plan for your life. Can I tell you a secret? Only you can do what God created you to do.

I have a challenge for you. Think of any task, any talent, anything that you can do, know that no-one else will do it just like you. There will never be a person who sings the way you do, tells jokes the way you do, drive, bake, speak, or even write the way you do. I know some tasks here may seem like things we take lightly, but they are an important part of the big picture.

You are not here by chance! God considered you and deliberately placed you here to fulfil a purpose. The Lord orchestrated your existence for such a time as this.

Even if it may seem like you are coming up on many obstacles and setbacks, don't give power to them by belabouring thoughts of inferiority; they can never define who you were created to be. Instead, use your mistakes, obstacles and setbacks to bring you closer to your destiny. You are the trademark of your Creator; you are God's masterpiece; the *imago dei*—image of God.

And if you need more proof, even the Scripture states that we were made a little lower than the angels. For me, this means that our worth is invaluable, it is priceless, it is of incalculable value and it is of inestimable worth. You are God's special child and don't ever forget it.

Now, if you do not know this, then you will never understand the value you bring to the tables you sit, the spheres you influence, the interactions you have, just by showing up. Wow! I don't know about you, but this absolutely blows my mind.

Understanding that you are fearfully and wonderfully made, having this ingrained in how you see yourself, makes it easier to understand that you have an inherent worth; a worth that requires you to be treated with dignity and respect. Use this principle to set the foundation for who you are. Once you do, then it will be easy for you to follow the other keys from this book.

Remember always—You are invaluable! Now pause and thank the Lord for making you, YOU!

Takeaway

Take your first step. Believe that you are fearfully and wonderfully made by our Lord who sees you as more than enough.

Inspirational Thought

"Before I formed you in the womb, I knew you; before you were born, I set you apart." (Jeremiah 1:5, NIV)

Introspection

What are the things I am good at? What is that one thing I can do, that no one can do like me?

Note to Self

_____

_____

_____

_____

_____

_____

_____

_____

_____

_____

_____

Step 2:
Who Are YOU?

Who are you? If I asked you this, what would your response be?

Would you instinctively start listing your biological attributes or would you mention some emotional attributes? However you describe yourself, you must understand three (3) things:

You are a spiritual being.

Knowing who you are involves knowing Jesus Christ as your Lord and Saviour. It is the Lord that created you and He knows the potential that exists within you. Gaining an understanding of who you are must be influenced by what the Lord has to say about you.

You are a holistic being.

You have many facets: emotional, spiritual, physical, rational and intellectual.

Your choice and way of existing are linked directly to your identity.

Your identity, as defined by the Oxford Learner's Dictionary, "is the characteristics, feelings or beliefs that make people different from others."

Whatever you do is tied to all these facets of you, the individual. Therefore, if you are playing, writing a book, having a conversation or just dancing, all these actions will be done based on the person you are, on your unique traits.

But, if you are still at a juncture where you are seeking external validation, then it's time to do some introspection. Ask yourself some questions to unearth your truth:

- When do I feel most fulfilled?
- How do I add value to the people in my life?
- What gifts or talents do I possess?
- What makes me most driven?
- What are my pet peeves?
- What annoys me most, and why?

- How well do I handle pressure?

- What traits do I want to possess?

From here, you will better understand the things you like and dislike, your strengths and weaknesses, your skills and talents, among other things.

If you are self-aware, it minimizes the need to gain external validation. When you get to this point, it soon becomes clear that even an act of someone giving you a compliment, serves simply as a confirmation of what you already know. Even your response will grow from one of sheer grate-fulness to 'thank you.' You'll never wait on persons to validate who you are.

When you know who you are, your core val-ues and beliefs are not easily shaken. Knowing who you are is the key to maintaining a positive self-esteem.

Anecdote

Have you ever thought about the value we place on diamonds in our society? More importantly, do you understand the process the diamond endures to become a diamond, and the effort invested to get it to its perfect state?

We find the diamond deep in the earth's core. Miners will go where there are diamonds. No matter how difficult the terrain, miners will risk their lives for this product they consider immensely valuable.

Similarly, show how invaluable you are. No amount of money in the world can equate your value and worth because you are priceless. No mineral can equate to who you are. No amount of clothing can compensate for the great treasure within you. Any hardships you may have endured, were part of your process to get you to the best version of yourself.

Takeaway

You don't need external validation. Know who you are!

Inspirational Thoughts

"I respect myself and insist upon it from every-body. And because I do it, I then respect everybody, too."—Maya Angelou

"I know who I am—I am the express image of the Father, the out-shinning of His glory. I am God's perfection of beauty. The fullness of God—the totality of His power—dwells in me. I am com-plete in Him. Hallelujah!" —Rhapsody of Realities

Introspection

a. How can I answer the question, "Who am I?" Write a paragraph which encapsulates who you are.

b. Write a letter to your future self, stating who you will be five (5) or ten (10) years from now. This will help with developing the person you as-pire to be.

Note to Self

Step 3:
Uniquely Made...No Comparison Needed

Do you believe you are one of a kind and absolutely remarkable?

Yes, you are! God peculiarly created each of us. Holding this truth helps us overcome our deepest fears. According to author, Marianne Williamson:

> Our deepest fear is not that we are inadequate. Our deepest fear is that we are powerful beyond measure. It is our light, not our darkness, that most frightens us. We ask ourselves, "Who am I to be brilliant, gorgeous, talented, fabulous? Actually, who are you not to be?" You are a child of God. Your playing small doesn't serve the world. There's nothing enlightened about shrinking so that other people won't feel insecure around you. We

are all meant to shine, as children do.

There will always be someone in a better circumstance than you and someone who is worse off. But we should never make comparisons. When we do, we begin to see life from another person's vantage point and not what was intended for us.

Think of an ostrich comparing itself to an eagle. The ostrich cannot fly, but doesn't it have many unique features and capabilities that the eagle has no claim to? National Geography records:

> Though they cannot fly, ostriches are fleet, strong runners. They can sprint up to 43 miles an hour and run over a distance of 31 miles an hour. They may use their wings as "rudders" to help them change direction while running. An ostrich's

powerful, long legs can cover 10 to 16 feet in a single stride. These legs can also be formidable weapons...They have sharp claws and beak and strong legs.

The eagle, on the other hand, has wings and can fly, soaring higher than all birds. The eagle is the bird of all birds because of its uniqueness. Because the eagle can soar, does it mean the ostrich isn't important and should be belittled? Of course not! The ostrich might not be able to soar, but it is extremely fast. It is the largest flightless bird that exists.

Takeaway

When you compare yourself with others, you belittle your own significance.

Inspirational Thought

"The reason why we struggle with insecurity is because we compare our behind the scenes with everyone else's highlight reel." —Steven Furtick

Introspection

In what ways have I compared myself with others? How can I not compare myself with others? What is unique to me?

Note to Self

_____

_____

_____

_____

_____

_____

_____

_____

Step 4:
Dare to Soar

What is hindering you from making that move to be the best version of you?

As a Christian, I do not subscribe to Charles Darwin's Evolution Theory. Neither do I believe we came in this world as blank slates—tabula rasa—as some psychologists say. We are created with innate gifts and talents which are inherent. They were downloaded in our make-up when the Lord created us.

Just as larvae transitions into caterpillars then metamorphose into butterflies; the butterflies are the end product of the evolution of larvae. Butterflies soar with such freedom to accomplish their goal. So too, you are a butterfly, waiting to take off to the next level.

In my interactions, I find people who constantly engage in active learning, seeking after new knowledge, enjoy life more. It's as if they always have something for which to look forward. They don't expend energy on negative thoughts, because their energy is always engaged in building themselves. This is an admirable approach to life.

Self-development is imperative, the onus is on us to make something of ourselves. You will find that the more you desire to achieve, the more you will be successful. There is a saying, "success is waiting for a comfortable place to stay." Work hard, engage in self-development, be consistent and success will find you.

Anecdote

I've always admired Brian for his passion for learning and exploration, and he never limited himself. At one point he was doing a course in interior decorating. When that was done, he started learning something in woodwork. Another time, he was learning another language and then to play an instrument.

The point is that the world is so dynamic and so we too, as individuals, should be just as dynamic to meet the changes that occur in life. If you take this approach, you will always be relevant! Dr. Spencer Johnson, author of "Who Moved My Cheese" examines the importance of being relevant and changing with the times. Positioning yourself is important as you navigate life. Challenge yourself by learning a skill, complete some short courses that can benefit you, learn a new language or even visit a new country to broaden your perspective on culture. Don't just exist; live.

Takeaway

You are a living organism; therefore, you won't always be at the same level—growth is inevitable.

Inspirational Thought

"One can never consent to creep when one feels the compulsion to soar."—Helen Keller

Introspection

What skill would I like to learn? Sign up for a course or learn a new skill at an institution near you. If you don't have the cash to do so, find a friend or person who can teach you something at a reasonable cost, or even for free. Plus, there are tons of low-cost and sometimes free courses available online. I also encourage you to hold yourself accountable by creating a timeline to meet these goals. Always remember what Zig Ziglar says, "If you aim at nothing, you will hit it every time."

See an example of a timeline on the next page, but get creative and find inspiration any-where you can. It's your timeline, so create something that will work perfectly for you.

Timeline for Short-Term Goals- January – November 2020
Personal Goals—Family, personal development, exercise, leisure

Example:

Spend 2 hours each Saturday with family

Complete a 3 months Interior Decorating Course

Go to the gym 4 times per week

Go on a cruise or to Paris

Note to Self

_____

_____

_____

_____

_____

_____

_____

_____

_____

Step 5:
Surround Yourself with People Who See Your Potential

When was the last time you did an inventory of your friends?

It's important to roll with the right crowd. There is an adage that says, "show me your friend and I will tell you who are." Surround yourself with persons who are not only good influencers, but also those you can learn from. Learning takes place every day and if you try to learn from those who have journeyed on similar paths before, then this can help you avoid some mistakes and navigate with much ease.

Your friends should be persons who can give sound advice and constructive criticism. Observe those who are consistently negative and know what place these persons should take in your life, if any. Be careful with whom you share your dreams. Not everyone knows how to handle persons who are always aspiring to better themselves.

Strive not to be liked, but to be valued by others. There is a big difference. It is not about being validated, instead; it is about having your core persons or inner circle who will help you reach your zenith. These are your staunch and dedicated cheerleaders, your friends, who will always be there.

Some friends may want for you to dim your light or lower your standards for their comfort. True friends will want the best for you as they do for themselves. I find this saying holds true, "...don't let someone dim your light, simply because it's shining in their eyes." If you are in a circle and this is your reality, then maybe it is time to change your circle. Author Nikki Rowe says it best, "Don't you dare feel guilty for letting those who dim your light, go. Not everyone you meet deserves a character in your story." You are in the business of bettering yourself, so if your friends cannot handle this, then they need to deal with their own insecurities and face the music.

So, what should you do? Get rid of toxic friendships and manipulators; these only hinder you. Be discerning and know with which group you should interact. Sometimes you just need to follow your instincts. After all, "Birds of a feather flock together"—individuals of the same sort or with similar tastes and interests will be found together.

Takeaway

The right supporter or well-wisher can aid your success. Be around people who value you and know your worth.

Inspirational Thoughts

"Surround yourself with good people. People who are going to be honest with you and look out for your best interest."—Derek Jeter

"Surround yourself with people and things that inspire you. Learn everything you can."—Jameela Jamil

Introspection

Do an inventory of the friends you have. Ask yourself: Am I a part of the right crowd? Are my friends and associates adding value to my life? Am I someone who adds value to my friends' lives?

Note to Self

_____

_____

_____

_____

_____

_____

_____

_____

_____

_____

Step 6:
Stay Away from Toxic People

How can I identify a toxic person?

We have the tendency to stay away from persons who are challenging. However, in the right context, these persons can assist us. Now, there is a difference between persons who challenge you to be the best you can be and those that literally sap every ounce of positive energy from your very being. These negative persons tend to be disrespectful, rude, manipulative, narcissistic and can be fault finders, magnifying even the smallest misstep. To them, nothing you do is good enough. I call these people dream killers. Their very aura wreaks negativity. Such persons do not deserve to be in your inner circle.

If you are saved, the Holy Spirit tells you how to deal with toxic persons. In some cases, the Holy Spirit may lead you to be the very solution to these persons' ills.

Those you should keep close are persons who share your dream, those who challenge you to see the full picture to getting you where you need to be (as seen in Step Five). These should be persons who constantly encourage you to aim higher.

It is often said that the eagle flies with eagles and not chickens, pigeons or ravens. They fly with other eagles who can soar and go the distance they do. This is a powerful reminder for you who are on a quest to better yourself. In Jamaica, there is also a saying, "birds of a feather flock together." This is important as we unknowingly adopt the characteristics and mannerisms of those with whom we associate frequently.

If you look in the mirror right now, I want for you to see that you are not a chicken or a raven; you are an eagle going places. You have everything inside you to survive and achieve all your goals. This is how you were created. There is a strong message in the way a person treats you, so don't allow anyone to downplay your worth.

Takeaway

Avoid negative persons.

Inspirational Thoughts

"Toxic people will pollute everything around them. Don't hesitate. Fumigate."—Mandy Hale"

"Until you let go of all the toxic people in your life, you will never be able to grow into your fullest potential. Let them go so you can grow."—DLQ

"Sometimes there are things in life that aren't meant to stay. Sometimes change may not be what we want. Sometimes change is what we need." —Don Bolena Jr.

Introspection:

What toxic relationships do I have in my life? What will I do after I have identified toxic persons and relationships?

Note to Self

_____

_____

_____

_____

_____

_____

_____

_____

_____

_____

_____

_____

_____

_____

Step 7:
Know Your Value and Worth

If someone were to ask "What is your value or worth?" What would your answer be?

It is often said that you should be and act the way you want to be treated. If you have high self-respect, then persons will treat you with respect. Radiate that which you want to see.

Not only should your mannerisms exude how you want to be treated, but you also have to look the part. Being well groomed and approachable is important. If you aren't aware, you are a package and you have to market your brand well. No one wants to associate with a brand that isn't appealing. Your brand should always represent who you are.

Anecdote

There is a lady I know. Whenever I am having a conversation with her, whether or not I want to listen, I am forced to listen. Maybe 'forced' is a strong word, but her mannerisms command my respect. The ironic thing is that this individual is small in stature, but her self-confidence is so tall and striking. She acts just as how she wants to be treated.

I remember the first time I met her. I was casually going about my business and she came to say something to me. I can't remember what it was at the time, but I remember being immediately engaged. Whatever she was saying was very convincing and her confidence, the manner in which she enunciated her words, really got my attention. Even though I was on my way, in somewhat of a rush, she got a fair share of my time because of all she represented.

When we know our value and worth, we will attract persons who will admire, love and appreciate us. Your value will never ever diminish because someone fails to see your worth.

Takeaway

If you don't know your value and worth, no one else will. Act the way you want others to treat you and market your brand well. Knowing and understanding your worth is priceless.

Inspirational Thought

"Because one believes in oneself, one doesn't try to convince others. Because one is content with oneself, one doesn't need others' approval. Because one accepts oneself, the whole world accepts him or her." —Everydaypower.com

Introspection

How can I enhance my brand? In what ways can this be done?

Note to Self

_____

_____

_____

_____

Step 8:
Respect Yourself

Would a bully prey on someone who would retaliate? Certainly not!

As human beings, we tend to prey on those we perceive to be weak. Bullying is found in every institution, and even as adults we may experience it. But the difference is whether or not you stand up for yourself. Now I'm not saying you are going to fight bullies that come your way, instead, let them know you are not afraid to defend your own honour.

Your self-confidence and self-respect should take the lead so that when you assert yourself, you command the respect of others.

While some of us are still learning how to radiate this kind of confidence, always keep in mind that the way you treat yourself, determines how others see you and ultimately treat you.

You may be doubtful, even hesitant, fearful that this is how it has been for so long, and lacking the boldness to tell people what you're really feeling. The thought may come, "Suppose it ends in a quarrel?" My answer to you is a resounding, "So what?" If you do the same things continuously, you can't expect a different result.

So, start simple. Make a list of your boundaries and let people know that your boundaries exist. It may mean literally speaking those words, or it could be a change in how you interact with them. Whatever you decide, stick to it.

Even while you figure out what your boundaries are, you may need to push beyond your fears, to stand up for yourself. I caution you though, be selective with how you defend yourself. They should be within reason. It would not be wise to start an argument to prove you are right, when the situation could be handled in a different and peaceful manner. As children of the Most High, whatever we do should reflect Christ.

Life can be challenging and living without respect and self-respect can make it even more challenging.

Anecdote

When I was younger, I didn't have the courage to stand up to anyone. I would usually allow people to say anything to me. I did not establish my boundaries. As I matured, I realized that I have every right to speak about my feelings and people need to know where I stand, what is acceptable and what is not. I must admit it took some time to be bold.

I recall distinctly an instance where a particular student in my grade four class told me I could not sing. I just accepted her opinion of my singing. I never raised any objection to her negative opinion of me. Her statement hurt me and still I remained silent. I didn't understand at that point that I could have refuted her opinion.

Here's another incident, but this is with the more mature, self-actualized me.

An agent had some documents I needed. He had them for quite some time, which should not have been the case. When I contacted him, he wasn't pleased and spoke in a tone I did not like, which was rather rude and disrespectful. Not appreciating the manner in which he spoke to me, I expressed my displeasure and commanded the respect due to me. The person quickly apologized and then his tone changed. Just like that, the situation was amicably resolved.

Notice the difference in both situations?

If you have not yet attained the boldness needed to express yourself, it isn't too late to do so. In your interactions and conversations, start by practising to gradually state your feelings. You may be timid to do so initially, but I have found the more you express yourself, the more likely you are to command the respect needed. People will eventually observe and admire your actions. Getting there isn't easy, but it can happen once you begin the journey.

To start establishing your boundaries:

- Know what brings you comfort and what does not.

- State your limits and let persons know what it is you want and don't want.

- Be vocal.

Author Wendy Mass, expresses it quite well, "The trick is that as long as you know who you are and what makes you happy, it doesn't matter how others see you." Therefore, what's important is how you see yourself.

You may feel you are weak and think that is how you will be. You are wrong. Each human be-ing was made with indomitable strength that needs to be unearthed. It is through building one's self esteem, being self-actualized, and hav-ing a positive self-concept, that you will find the strength within. When this strength is found, the unimaginable becomes a reality, the insurmount-able becomes surmountable, the unachievable becomes achievable, the unattainable becomes attainable, and the unreachable becomes reachable. There is no limit to what you can do. Why not start now by respecting who you are? You owe it to yourself.

Takeaway

Respect the person you are by setting your boundaries.

Inspirational Thought

"Respect first emanates from you, it will then be seen by others and replicated."—Andrine Tul-loch-Francis

Introspection

In what ways can I command respect? How can I set boundaries? In what ways can I show I am not weak?

Note to Self

_____

_____

_____

_____

_____

_____

_____

_____

_____

_____

_____

_____

_____

_____

Step 9:
Positive Thoughts Only

I am capable of excelling!

I can do all things through Christ who strengthens me!

I can do this!

I will be the best version of myself!

What thoughts are you harbouring about yourself?

The key to possessing high self-esteem is to consistently maintain positive thoughts. Scientists show that persons who maintain positive thoughts, "can strongly influence our level of happiness and lead us to flourish both physically and psychologically."[1]

Do not make negative statements about yourself. Even if negative statements pop up in your head, counter them with at least three positive thoughts about yourself. Each morning, look in your mirror and remind yourself of the good attributes and characteristics you possess. If this is done perpetually, the brain will constantly convey positive messages. Positive thinking is important.

Positive thoughts create a healthy mind. Science tells us that the neuron is the basic working unit of the brain, a specialized cell, within the nervous system, designed to transmit information to other nerve cells, muscle or gland cells. Therefore, it is important we consistently transmit positive thoughts to our neurons. Healthy minds yield favourable results. Our minds possess immeasurable success. Why not tap into it and unearth the greatness that lies within you!

Author and Educator Consultant, Kendra Cherry, in her article, "Understanding the Psychology of Positive Thinking," cites the Harvard Gazette which states that, "Positive thinking can aid in stress management and even plays an important role in your overall health and well-being." [2]

What does positive thinking have to do with your health? Everything. Our overall health and well-being are necessary if we are to maintain a positive self-esteem. A positive self-esteem is therefore contingent on our mental health. Both are correlated and mutually inclusive.

You may therefore be thinking, what is positive thinking? Cherry quotes Martin Seligman, Psychologist (2006), in her article, "Positive thinking does not necessarily mean avoiding or ignoring the bad things; instead, it involves making the most of the potentially bad situations, trying to see the best in other people, and viewing yourself and your abilities in a positive light."

So, viewing who you are, and your abilities in a positive light is extremely important. Harbouring positive thoughts should always be a top priority on your to-do list.

Start by creating positive thoughts. Here are a few ideas.

Surround yourself with persons who can objectively highlight your good qualities. This reinforcement helps in maintaining the right attitude.

Avoid Self-Sabotaging Thoughts

These are thoughts that admit defeat before you even begin a task. Thoughts such as: "I can't sing and...., I don't have the cash, I don't have the ability to..., I can't write, no one knows me.... etc. We all, at some point in our lives, have these thoughts. As soon as you feel them surfacing, immediately counter them with something positive. For example, "I cannot do this," can be countered with, "I have everything inside me to be successful, others have done it before, so can I."

Try self-talking.

Self-talk is a concept that is important when we consider positive thoughts. As explained by Kimberly Holland, Health, Travel and Lifestyle Writer, self-talk is "your internal dialogue. It is influenced by your subconscious mind, and it reveals your thoughts, beliefs, questions and ideas." The nature of self-talk can be negative or positive, based on what you garnered in your formative years. It can be encouraging or distressing.

According to Holland, the benefits of positive self-talk and a more optimistic outlook can have health benefits which include: increased vitality, greater life satisfaction, improved immune function, reduced pain, better cardiovascular health, better physical well-being, less stress and distress. Holland further states, "Research suggests people with positive self-talk may have mental skills that allow them to solve problems, think differently and be more efficient at coping with hardships or challenges," thereby reducing stress and anxiety. So, if you are someone who realizes your self-talk is more negative than positive, then there is the need to change this. Fortunately, negative self-talk can be changed once the individual is deliberate about it.

How can you change negative self-talk? First, identify negative thinking, says Holland. Here are some scenarios of positive and negative self-talk.

Negative: I can't do this.

Positive: I will try to accomplish this task, though it seems difficult.

Negative: I can't speak well and everyone will laugh at me if I do the speech.

Positive: I am capable and strong. So, what if others laugh? I will do my best. I can grow from the experience.

Negative: I failed miserably. Now I look bad.

Positive: I am proud of myself for trying. I gave it my all. I have learnt from this failure. I will not repeat the same mistakes next time.

A part of your self-talk should be you complimenting yourself on the way you look. Never be afraid to compliment yourself. Remember, knowing and understanding your worth is priceless. Your worth is never, ever contingent on the opinions of others. Rather, your worth should be entrenched in your schema, so incorporated in your very DNA that you are a masterpiece. If you remember this, then you will have no problem with engaging yourself with positive self-talk.

Be deliberate and intentional about following Philippians 4:8 (KJV) which urges us to think on "Whatsoever things are true, whatsoever things are honest, whatsoever things are just, whatsoever things are pure, whatsoever things are lovely, whatsoever things are of good report; if there be any virtue or praise, we should think on these things." This too will help you to deepen your fellowship with God.

Take Away

 Consistently engage in positive self-talk.

Inspirational Thoughts

"Our subconscious minds have no sense of humor, play no jokes, and cannot tell the difference between reality and an imagined thought or image. What we continually think about eventually will manifest in our lives."—Sidney Madwed

"She knew the power of her mind and so programmed it for success." —Carrie Green

"What we think determines what happens to us, so if we want to change our lives, we need to stretch our minds." —Wayne Dyer

How you see yourself determines how others see you.

Introspection

Look in the mirror and state five (5) positive attributes about yourself. Repeat this daily.

Note to Self

_____

_____

_____

_____

_____

_____

_____

_____

_____

_____

_____

_____

_____

_____

_____

_____

[1] Malcolm, Lynne "Scientific evidence points to importance of positive thinking". Posted Wed 17 Jun 2015, 5:00pm Updated Fri 19 Jun 2015, 11:08am. Accessed March 7, 2020.
https://www.abc.net.au/radionational/programs/allinthemind/the-scientific-evidence-for-positive-thinking/6553614

[2] Kendra, Cherry citing How power of positive thinking works. The Harvard Gazette. Published December 7, 2016

Step 10:
Love Yourself—Even Your Flaws

W hat flaws have you identified about yourself?

We can be so hard on ourselves. Oftentimes, we are really our greatest critic. Though we have flaws, it doesn't mean we can't appreciate the positive attributes we possess. Flaws, for the purpose of this book, are defined as a fault or weakness in a person's character. I might add that as long as these flaws are not sinful, that is offensive to God and man, there is always something positive we can look at.

So, what should you do?

Make the choice daily to focus on the positives of your life, embracing every part of your body, mannerisms and attribute.

Think about a mango that falls on the ground. Chances are, the area that first hits the ground will be bruised, it may get soft. The mango may even have worms. If you have a great liking for mangoes, even if all three (3) flaws are present, that won't stop you from eating and tantalizing your taste buds. And after you've eaten the fruit, will you focus on all the flaws or reminisce about how good it was? More often than not, it would be the latter. The juiciness (succulence), sweetness and other things would race to your mind and that would make up the experience you recall.

As you ponder on this mango scenario, similarly, you can look at the entire package that epitomizes or encapsulates you, the individual. Our flaws are not there to impede our progress. Instead, they are present to propel us to be a better version of ourselves. Your inadequacies and shortcomings do not define who you are, neither should you equate them with who you are. If you look through God's eyes, you are His masterpiece and you should think nothing less of yourself.

It is also important to laugh at yourself at times. We too easily forget that life should be enjoyed with all the trappings and frills that come with it. It's ok if there are days you relax and think about the lighter things of life. Do as the song says, "Smile awhile and give your face a rest."

So, feel free to laugh uncontrollably at yourself and reminisce. Life is difficult, but there are wonderful moments as well. Can you think of a moment when you did something so hilarious and you wondered how did this thing happen? Yes, I am sure you are smiling now. It was so funny and it made you see another layer of yourself. All of this includes embracing your flaws.

Anecdote

I had a colleague whom I admired so much because of her ability to freely laugh at herself. She would often recollect the times she did something crazy or something that was just simply hilarious. I admired her confidence when she shared the stories. They certainly made me laugh to think of the things she did.

I think one of her most hilarious moments was about heading downtown Kingston from Marescaux Road. As a Jamaican, we know that it is the norm for taxis to stop at that spot and pick up passengers. On this particular day, a car stopped and my friend headed straight to the front seat. Another female was trying to get the same seat.

My friend, fully confident, looked at the lady with such disdain, appalled that she dared to vie for the same seat, which she clearly was going in. By the time my friend settled in, the driver told her that he was not a taxi. It was only then that my friend realized that the other passenger was the driver's significant other. The driver opted to take her to her destination still, since she was already in the car, but, feeling rather cute and embarrassed, my friend came out of the taxi, long before she reached her destination.

But, recalling the story, she was ecstatic with laughter.

She showed me how to embrace who I am and accept that mistakes will be made. From time to time, you will do silly things, but it is a part of life.

It is in Christ that most of the confidence that has true and lasting value lies. Without Christ, we can do nothing.

Takeaway

Your flaws are present on your journey not to sidetrack or derail your purpose.

Inspirational Thought

"God, grant me the serenity to accept the things I cannot change, courage to change the things I can, and wisdom to know the difference."
— Reinhold Niebuhr

Introspection

What areas in my life have I not accepted? How can I accept my flaws? What can I do to better myself?

Note to Self

_____

_____

_____

_____

_____

_____

_____

_____

_____

_____

Step 11:
High Self-Esteem, Not Narcissism

I am capable of excelling!

I can do all things through Christ who strengthens me!

I can do this!

I will be the best version of myself!

How can I differentiate between high self-esteem and being self-absorbed?

We have established that having positive self-esteem is good. But we have to be careful not to become too self-absorbed. There is a very thin line between being self-aware and being narcissistic. Having positive thoughts about one's self is good, but when we go overboard, it becomes a problem. Take a look at this conversation:

Nicole: Hey Jasmine! I'm so glad to see you. I had such a hard day at work today and just really need someone to help me talk through some things.

Jasmine: Girrrrlllll... guess what?! Tom said he wanted to take me out. (Screams frantically!) I can't wait. Tom finally saw that I'm all that and more. I mean, winning personality, check and am absolutely gorgeous.

Nicole: That's really lovely. Sounds like things are moving in the right direction. But Jasmine, I'm trying to tell you about my day. It was such a...

Jasmine: (... chimes in before Nicole could even finish her thought.) Don't worry about that man. That happens sometime. Anyway, Tom says it's a surprise. I really can't wait. He says I should dress formal. I wonder what I should wear...

And Jasmine carries on, unaware of Nicole's sadness.

Now, let's do a post mortem on the conversation:

- Who was being inconsiderate and slightly narcissistic?

- What undesirable behaviours were seen in this interaction?

- What could have been done differently?

- Did the conversation almost feel like a monologue to you?

Throughout the conversation, Jasmine's attention was focused on herself and not her friend. Friendships should have some level of reciprocity, empathy and consideration. The Bible expresses it quite well, "A man who has friends must himself be friendly."

Have you ever known someone who, every conversation you have with the individual, they speak about themselves? Every conversation, no matter what the initial topic was, transitions to what they do, their accomplishments and everything about them? This is the definition of being self-absorbed. Psychologists' research posits that persons who are consistently self-centred have inadequacies they are trying to fill. Avoid such persons and do not become that person.

Remember, when you engage in conversations, share some of the spotlight; humility and modesty are fragments of having a positive self-image. Practise striking the balance—knowing when to and when not to toot your own horn. Being confident in who you are, doesn't mean you go on a never-ending quest to show people you are of value and worth. Your character and attributes will speak for themselves.

Takeaway

Know when to speak of yourself and choose the appropriate moments to do so.

Inspirational Thought

"The main condition for the achievement of love is the overcoming of one's narcissism." —Erich Fromm

Introspection

When I speak, are my words self-absorbing? Do I always think I must be in the limelight? How can I create a balance in my conversations?

Note to Self

_____

_____

_____

_____

_____

_____

_____

_____

_____

_____

_____

Step 12:
Maintaining Close Fellowship with God

What is your relationship with God like? This question is pertinent to every stage of your growth.

Jeremiah 1: 5 states, "Before I formed you in the womb, I knew you, before you were born, I set you apart... (NIV)" The Lord knows why you were sent here, for a specific purpose. It is through maintaining the right fellowship with God that you will truly be who you were created to be. The Lord knows what skills and talents you were created to embrace. Maintaining fellowship with God can help to empower who you are and build the right perception you should have of yourself.

I always encourage persons to go back where it all started. Consider the Lord the architect who created the blueprint. If there is ever a problem or situation, it is the architect of the building who can tell you where the safety features, strengths and secret passage ways are. Similarly, the Lord knows every detail about you. The scripture tells us that He, God, knows the very hairs on our head and He knows everything about us. Scripture further explains in Psalm 139:8-10, wherever we go He, God, is there. Isaiah 44:24 (KJV) states, "The LORD that made thee, and formed thee from the womb...."

The Lord knew there were days we would feel down and so He inspired man to write the Bible. From here, you can draw your strength when you are weak. When you feel despondent, it is your 'go to' book. It makes a world of difference.

Allowing the Lord to be completely in control of your life is a move in the right direction. Self-esteem that is anchored on Christ Jesus will stand the test of time, crisis and adverse situations. If God has complete control over your heart, it is a beautiful garden for Him to plant His seeds of righteousness and all the other things that come with knowing the Lord Jesus Christ. As author Donnette Norman states, "We must understand that self is an affront to God." Whatever we do should be focused on the Lord. Proverbs 4: 23 (ESV) states, "Keep your heart with all vigilance, for from it flow the springs of life." What are the springs of life (the King James Version translates it as the "issues of life") it is all holy desires, all good counsels, and all just works. Only the Lord can truly give us the self-esteem needed through Jesus Christ our Lord. Acknowledging Him and submitting to His way helps us to receive abundant life.

Anecdote

It wasn't until January 2005, that I truly knew the Lord for myself. Prior to this, I was a somewhat shy person. I didn't have an identity and I was easily swayed by my friends. After my encounter with Christ, many things about me changed. I started learning who I was, my self- esteem blossomed and I was able to make the connection with what my purpose here on earth is. I try daily to crucify self so that God's word can be manifested in my life. I thank God for the change that He has made in me. Thank you, Lord!

Takeaway

God has the blueprint for your life, so trust Him to construct the empowered you.

Inspirational Thought

"For I know the plans I have for you," declares the Lord, "plans to prosper you and not to harm you, plans to give you hope and a future." —Jeremiah 29:11, NIV

Introspection

What can I do to spend more time with my Creator?

Note to Self

_____

_____

_____

_____

_____

_____

_____

_____

_____

_____

_____

_____

_____

_____

Step 13:
Affirm Yourself Daily

How often do you affirm yourself?

To affirm means to state emphatically or publicly. Many times we focus on the negatives. We are not ashamed to say them out loud. Even when we fail, we believe that our failures define us. This, my friend, is very far from the truth.

Actually, our failures give us experiences so we can become better versions of ourselves. Usain Bolt in the 2004 Athens Olympics did not finish well. In the 200m, he did not even complete his race. He learned from the experience and in 2008, 2012 and 2016, Usain won all his events at the Olympics.

This is one of the more popular examples but there are many more persons who have failed and then came back better the next time. One of the things they did was to affirm themselves.

Dr. Charmaine Johnson-Garwood is another example of triumph after failure. She shared her story on Profile, then hosted by the talented journalist Ian Boyne, on April 30, 2017. Dr. Johnson-Garwood spoke of some hard times and how she went back to school at thirty-two, only then completing her subjects in General Certificate of Education (G.C.E.). This was after dropping out of school because of pregnancy at 16. Since then, Dr. Johnson-Garwood acquired two master's degrees and two doctoral degrees, specialising in Clinical and Industrial Psychology with focus on Trauma for Children and Adolescence.

She experienced much at a young age. In addition to being pregnant at 16, she was stabbed in her two lungs, and she witnessed the death of her mother. But Dr. Johnson-Garwood did not see her life as a linear path. Life gives many lessons which do not necessarily go in a straight direction. You may experience curves, bends, hills even mountains. She opines that, "you cannot let your obstacles be your goal." She went on further to explain, "Life will throw you curve balls but if we get fixated on why this should not have happened, you end up losing the opportunity to make something happen." This is the approach we should take to navigate life. She was determined and so she developed the capacity to overcome obstacles. Is there something in Dr. Johnson-Garwood's story that resonates with you?

Too often, we seek affirmation from others. We should not. Cultivate an attitude where even if no one affirms you, you will be your number one fan. Be your biggest cheerleader!

How? Each morning, start with your self-talk. Look in the mirror and speak only positive things that will empower you. The more you affirm yourself, the more you find that your words will become a reality. The Bible states that life and death are in the power of the tongue. Love yourself and emphatically highlight your strengths.

In the past you might have been hard on yourself, allowed persons to walk over you, treat you horribly and other negative things. Now is the time to apologize to yourself. Yes, you can. You can look in the mirror and apologize for all the negative things you have said and done to yourself, the things you still have not forgiven yourself for or you can write an apology letter to yourself. Whichever you feel will be most meaningful. After you have completed the apology, then affirm who you are. You can do this!

Takeaway

The more you affirm yourself, the more you will love who you are. Daily tell yourself five (5) positive things about yourself.

Inspirational Thought

"Death and life are in the power of the tongue, and those who love it will eat its fruits." (Proverbs 18:21, ESV).

Introspection

What five (5) things can I declare daily about my-self?

Note to Self

_____

_____

_____

_____

_____

_____

_____

_____

_____

_____

_____

Step 14:
Step Out in Confidence

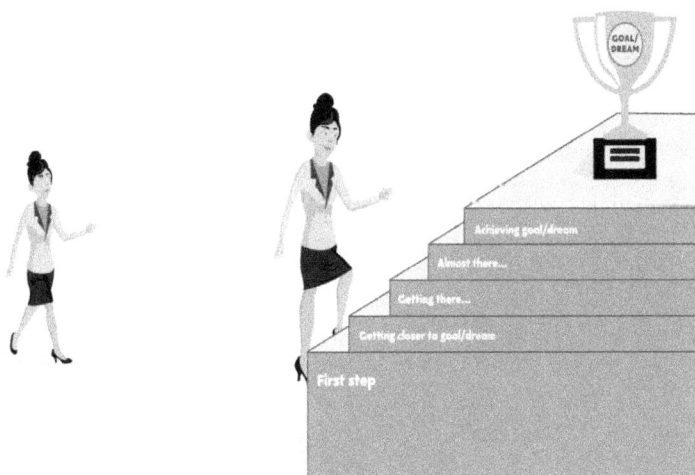

The steps shown, from bottom to top:
- First step
- Getting closer to goal/dream
- Getting there...
- Almost there...
- Achieving goal/dream

GOAL/DREAM

Why don't you just step out and do you?

Confidence is something you acquire during your sojourn here on earth. For me, I was a scaredy cat—always afraid. I thank God for both my parents who saw that there was something in me. My mom would always encourage me to participate in church activities. Her encouragement propelled me to do well. My dad, whenever bad things happened in my life, he would tell me to write ten (10) positive things about myself and say them in the mirror daily. Little did I know that the things both my parents were doing were affirming and building my self-confidence. My mother did not allow "I can't" to be a part of my vocabulary. She would repeatedly say, "I know my daughter and you can do anything you put your mind to."

Your reality may not include supportive parents, but you can still find other ways to take on the persona of being confident. Watch movies with the persona being confident, emulate persons in your social milieu that portray confidence, trust in the Lord to boost your self-esteem. As they say sometimes, you will have to "fake it before you make it". Step out and show the world that you have a right to be here. With confidence growing, you'll soon learn that more can be accomplished. You'll be more prepared to take the opportunities life has to offer. With Christ, all things are possible!

Takeaway

Exude confidence when you step out. Believe that you can do anything to which you put your mind.

Inspirational Thoughts

"If you don't have confidence in yourself, you are twice defeated in the race of life. With confidence, you have won even before you have started." — Marcus Garvey

"You have to expect things of yourself before you can do them." — Michael Jordan

Introspection

What opportunities have I missed? What opportunities are before me that I can now pursue?

Note to Self

_____

_____

_____

_____

_____

_____

_____

_____

Part II:
Maintaining High Self-Esteem

I am capable of excelling!

I can do all things through Christ who strengthens me!

I can do this!

I will be the best version of myself!

Self-Esteem Guide Table

This list is not exhaustive. You may identify and add other attributes.

	High Self-Esteem and Statements Exemplifying Attributes	Low-Self-Esteem and Statements Exemplifying Attributes
Characteristics/ Attributes	*Self-Respect* (Please don't speak to me in such an offensive manner, I would prefer you lower your voice and state what you are saying without being condescending.)	*Heavy Self-Criticism* (I can't seem to do anything right).
	Self-Love (I didn't do so well on my exam but I gave it my best shot. Next time I will do much better.)	*Hypersensitivity to Criticism* (Why do you always pick on me?)
	Feels Good in Own Skin (I love my body. God created me and I am fearfully and wonderfully made.)	*Chronic indecision* (Should I choose blue or green, or should it be pink? Can someone help me choose please?)
	Acknowledges Compliments (Thank you, I really worked hard on this speech).	*People-Pleasing* (Sure, I will do whatever you desire.)
	Focuses on Strengths (I am a good motivator and friend.)	*Feelings of Insignificance* (I feel so out of place here, I don't belong.)
General Mannerisms		
	Very Vocal / vocal awareness	Not Vocal
	Achieves Goals / Goal-setter/ Go-getter	Rarely Aspires towards a Goal
	Confident	Lacks Self-Confidence

Now, that you have seen the examples, add your statements showing high or low self-esteem using the table below.

	High Self-Esteem	Low Self-Esteem
Characteristics /Attributes		

Poem
What do I see?

I look in the mirror

Once there was trepidation, fear, pity and so many other negative words.

But now I see promise, worth, value and endless possibilities

In spite of my imperfections I have commonalities

Commonalities with great persons

Michelle Obama, Maya Angelou, Rosa Parks just to name a few

It is the story of what's new

So, if you don't see what I see

Then I suggest you take another view

Your negativity will not dictate my progress

So, deal with the process

This is the new and improved me

No longer will I procrastinate or delay

Because I am not the ordinary woman I used to be

I am rising, rising to new heights

Rising with might

Rising so the world can see the

Phenomenal me.

I look in the mirror, this is what I now see

Now as you look in the mirror, what do you see?

—Written by Andrine Tulloch-Francis
(December 12, 2018)

Daily To-Do List

A positive self-esteem needs to be nurtured. Here are some daily tips to practise:

1. Each day, look in the mirror and affirm yourself. Start with ten (10) positive things about yourself.

2. Find Scriptures that say who you are in Christ and declare them daily. Aim for a minimum of five (5).

3. Learn a new skill.

4. Challenge yourself to go before large audiences and sing, speak, do anything.

5. When asked to participate in an event, gladly accept the task.

6. Pray for the Lord to give you boldness.

7. Interact with persons that have high self-esteem, not narcissists.

8. Consistently evaluate how to value your self-worth.

9. Write ten (10) strengths people say you possess.

10. Find a trustworthy mentor, who can help you at the various stages of your self-esteem journey.

Daily Declarations

Some daily declarations you speak over your life unapologetically:

I am smart!

I am talented!

I have a God- given right to be here

I am phenomenal!

I am successful!

I am not here by chance

I have everything inside me to be successful

I am who God says I am

I am created for greatness

I was never a mistake!

I am a winner!

Whatever I do shall prosper

I am intelligent

I am fearfully and wonderfully made

I am victorious, no longer will I have self-sabotaging thoughts neither will I allow others to dissuade, disrupt or derail what I was created to be

I am God's most prized possession, the apple of His eyes

I am unique, no one can do the things I do

I am a survivor

I deserve all the good things that come my way

I deserve respect

I am invaluable.

"I know who I am. I am the expressed image of the Father, the out-shinning of His glory. I am God's perfection of beauty. The fullness of God—the totality of His power—dwells in me. I am complete in Him. Hallelujah!" (from Rhapsody of Realities)

Conclusion

Your Self-Esteem Is Greater Than Past Abuse!

There are many things in life which have happened, some good and others not so good.

You may have been abused emotionally, physically or sexually at a tender age, during your adolescent years or even as an adult. This however is not a death sentence, though it is a difficult journey. Maybe you have never confided in anyone about the situation because you may be embarrassed, you don't want persons to feel sorry for you, you may even be afraid of what others may think or maybe you just don't believe it's good to be vulnerable.

Research has shown that it is good to speak especially when we are in pain. Speaking is cathartic, it helps to relieve pain that we have suppressed. Sometimes bottled pain can lead to other complications which can be hazardous to our health. I am not saying you should tell everyone your problem; however, it is good to share with a mature and trustworthy person, the issues you go through. You never know how beneficial speaking to someone can be.

Many times, persons who have been abused put up a wall to avoid relationships, sometimes they mask their pain by working hard. Some may become maladaptive and some may even be functional, yet they suffer silently. In many instances these persons become recluse or introverts because they are hurting and grappling with abuse endured.

It's going to be difficult but you will have to make a deliberate effort to turn this negative situation into a positive one. Don't be hard on yourself, no one deserves abuse and it is not your fault! Garner the courage to speak to someone who can really help you; a friend, pastor, guidance counsellor or psychologist. These persons are trained to assist with the healing process. When you speak, you are standing up to your abuser and you are gradually being healed in the process. Some thoughts that may surface are:

How do I know this will work?

I have kept this secret for so many years. Who will believe me?

Will there be a change?

Change will come once you believe it will and your healing may even assist others who have experienced and suffered similarly. After all, as humans, we were never created to exist on our own. We are all interdependent. We genuinely need each other to survive and your example may be the light that someone else may have been looking out for.

So, be the best version of yourself by giving yourself a chance to really live and break free from your abuser's hold. Be a victor and overcomer! Fight that need for emotional independence which can lead to maladaptive and destructive behaviour, hindering you from being the best version of yourself. Having a positive self-esteem can help you to know what beneficial actions to take. Being quiet about something that is harmful can be detrimental.

I encourage you also not to allow this period of your journey to define you. You are more than your experiences. Your experiences can illustrate how to deal or cope with situations but they never dictate who you are.

My sisters, you are not alone in this journey of life. May you see the need to relieve yourself of the burden you have been carrying for days, months or years. You have the right to sleep freely, worry less or not to be agitated by triggers which your attacker created. We were not created to carry burdens and guilt. Instead, we were created to live a life progressing and developing daily, reaching the zenith of our potential -a life centered around massive growth and improvement. Free yourself from the bondage of your abuser, and make your indelible mark here on earth. You've got this and it is going to be ok.

I created this acrostic R-I-S-E as a test to assist you through this difficult time. Do try to complete for a minimum of 30 days and journal the benefits. The change starts in your mind; a powerful tool that is waiting to be effectively used. Don't conform to your past, but train your mind to deliberately achieve the best version of you.

Release yourself by speaking to someone about the abuse you have experienced or are experiencing.

Inscribe your feelings in a journal. After many days, look back and see how your journey has been progressing and identify behaviors that you have developed since abuse and do an inventory of which are positive and negative. With assistance, rid yourself of negative behaviours or habits.

Step towards healing by declaring daily, 'this situation will not cripple my progress or growth'. Stop focusing on the abuse and redirect thoughts on where you would want to be.

Explain to yourself daily, 'I will no longer be a victim of this situation' and use this negative situation as a launching pad for a life-changing and phenomenal transformation.

Takeaway

Negative situations or events can propel me to be the best version of myself.

Inspirational Thought

"We become what we think about... The human mind is the last great unexplored continent on the earth......We are the subtotal of our thoughts." —Earl Nightingale

Introspection

- What am I going to do about my past?
- What deliberate and intentional steps can I take to step pass my past?
- How can I nurture a positive self-esteem?

Note to Self

_____

_____

_____

_____

_____

_____

_____

_____

Afterword

So, you have read the book.

I hope it spoke to the person you are meant to be. You were created to think highly of yourself. Where you are now may not be where you should be: that job; that relationship you have endured, knowing you deserve better; that promotion, that house, (yes that house); that spot in the school play; that career change, that gentleman you want to date; whatever the situation, now is the time to pursue it.

There might have been some obstacles or challenges along the way: being in an abusive relationship or maybe even being a victim of sexual abuse, losing that job that gave great monetary compensation or you simply allowed an opportunity to pass you by. Whatever the challenge or obstacle, you no longer have to allow the things in your past to keep you down. With Christ that which seems impossible is possible.

Push forward, hold your head high and be deliberate to think valuable and positive thoughts about yourself. Decide in this moment, this instant, to change what is, to what should be. You, yes, you are the only person who has the power to dig deep and provide the atmosphere that is needed for thinking highly of yourself. It is not your parents, siblings, spouse, abuser, teacher or friend. It is you. So why not start that journey right now?

Feeling good about yourself should be the norm. It can be detrimental and disadvantageous to have low self-esteem. With positive self-esteem, phenomenal changes can take place in your life leading to a happier and better you. Step forward... you've got this!

Book Reviews

Book reviews are the life blood of authors. It is social proof. If buyers don't see reviews online, they won't buy the book. Please leave an honest review of this book wherever you bought this book online. Thank you.

You can also send feedback to the author at atullochfrancis2@gmail.com.

Acknowledgements

I want to thank the Lord for inspiring me to complete this book. Special mention to Celia Neufville and Nikisha Smith for the initial rounds of editing and practical suggestions given. For the many times I called you and the assistance you freely gave, I am grateful for your support.

Donnette Norman, Roshelle Jackson, Candice Allen and Dr. Nsombi Jaja for your well-crafted reviews, thank you.

Temiloluwa Adeoye and Nicola Brown, thanks for putting on the 'final touches', making the book ready to be consumed by its readers. To all who played a part in making this book a reality, I sincerely appreciate your contribution.

To my husband, Nevroy, for believing in my dream, thank you. My parents, you have been my constant support. Thank you for the many lessons taught which helped to inspire this book.

In advance, I would like to thank anyone who will take the time to read my work. It is my hope that the thoughts expressed can serve as guiding principles for your lives. You have helped to make one of my dreams come to fruition and I will be forever grateful.

Every Blessing,

Andrine

References

Baumeister. Roy F., Jennifer D. Campbell, Joachim I. Krueger and Kathleen D. Vohs. "Does High Self-Esteem Cause Better Performance, Interpersonal Success, Happiness, or Healthier Lifestyles?" Sage Journals Psychological Science in the Public Interest. May 1, 2003. https://journals.sagepub.com/doi/10.11 11/1529-1006.01431. Retrieved May 23, 2020.

Chaston, Karen. "Developing self-esteem is key to your success." The Business Woman Media. September 16, 2014. https://.www.thebusiness womanmedia.com/developing-self-esteem-key-success/. Retrieved February 2, 2020.

Cherry, Kendra. Medically reviewed by Snyder Carly. Understanding the Psychology of Positive Thinking. November 26, 2019. https://www.verywellmind.com/what-is-positive-thinking-2794772#citation-1. Retrieved February 2, 2020.

Holland, Kimberly. Medically Reviewed by Timo-
thy J. Legg. "Positive Self-Talk: How Talking to
yourself is a good thing" Healthline. October
17, 2018. https://www.healthline.com/health/
positive-self-talk. Retrieved February 2, 2020

Malcolm, Lynne. "Scientific Evidence for positive
thinking"abc.net.au. June 2015.
https://www.abc.net.au/radionational/progra
ms/allinthemind/the-scientific-evidence-for-
positive-thinking/6553614. Retrieved February
2, 2020.

National Geography.
https://www.nationalgeographic.com/animals
/birds/o/ostrich/. Retrieved February 2, 2020.

About the Author

Andrine Tulloch hails from the beautiful, pristine parish of Portland. She is one of the praise and worship leaders at her church, a motivational speaker, Christian and wife. She is a proud alumna of the prestigious Titchfield High School and a graduate of the University of the West Indies, Mona, where she completed both undergraduate and postgraduate degrees.

As a firm believer in empowering the next generation, Andrine has been an educator at the secondary level for over 15 years. She currently works at the St. Hugh's High School.

Andrine recognizes the importance of a positive self-esteem particularly in this technological age. She believes it is important for women to embrace who they are—be unapologetic about having positive thoughts—and that a woman who knows her worth can accomplish anything with Christ.

Her mantra is taken from Luke 1: 37 (KJV) "For with God nothing shall be impossible."

Andrine maintains that each woman has the *power to create, nurture and transform*. She believes the words of Steve Maraboli, "The empowered woman is powerful beyond measure and beautiful beyond description." Andrine empowers women through motivation and encouragement.

Note: For speaking engagements, conferences and workshops, contact the author at atullochfrancis2@gmail.com.

LinkedIn: Andrine Tulloch-Francis

Instagram: atullochfrancis

www.ingramcontent.com/pod-product-compliance
Lightning Source LLC
La Vergne TN
LVHW021452080426
835509LV00018B/2249